ARNOLD JANSSEN

ARNOLD JANSSEN

1837–1909

A PICTORIAL

BIOGRAPHY

Photographs
and Documentation
from His Life

by Franz-Josef Eilers
and Heinz Helf

Translated from
ER SÄTE GOTTES WORT: ARNOLD JANSSEN 1837–1909

Acknowledgements:

Photographs and Documentation: Bernward Mankau –
6, 8, 10, 12, 13, 16, 17, 20–26, 30, 31, 32, 35, 36, 40,
46, 47, 49, 55, 58, 65, 90, 91, 93

Heinz Helf – 9, 11, 27, 34, 36, 39, 53, 61, 62, 66, 72,
99, 102

Archives 'Kirche und Leben', Münster – 28, 30

Archivio Fotografico P.I.M.E., Milano – 45

Felici, Rome – 100, 101

Sr. M. Alacoque, SSpS de ad. perp. – 75

KLM Aerocarto, Holland – 74

Archiv Steyl – others

Grafic Art: Karl Höller – 56

Maps: Norbert A. Ciernioch

ARNOLD JANSSEN: 1837–1909
A PICTORIAL BIOGRAPHY;
Photographs and Documentation from his Life
By Franz-Josef Eilers and Heinz Helf – Nettetal:
Steyler Verlag – Wort u. Werk, 1987
ISBN 3-8050-0189-4

ISBN 3-8050-0189-4

2nd. edition 1987
©1987 Steyler Verlag – Wort und Werk, 4054 Nettetal 2
All Rights Reserved
Publisher: Editorial Verbo Divino
            31200 ESTELLA (Navarra)
            SPAIN

ISBN 84-7151-557-1
Dep. Legal: NA. 1.562-1987
Printed and Pound by: Gráficas Lizarra, S.L.
                       Ctra. de Tafalla, Km. 1
                       ESTELLA (Navarra)
                       SPAIN
Design & Lay-out: Norbert A. Ciernioch

ARNOLD JANSSEN

This book aims to record through pictures and text the life and deeds of Arnold Janssen, one of the great Catholic missionaries of our time. Many photographs were taken during his lifetime; others are of the environs in which he lived and worked. The text includes excerpts from his letters, memoirs and publications. Occasionally, contemporaries such as his brother Wilhelm (Brother Juniperus, OFM Cap) are quoted.
All quotations are printed in ordinary type and background material in italics.

On 17 August 1861 Arnold Janssen celebrated his First Mass. The scripture lesson of that Mass, "Do not forget: thin sowing means thin reaping; the more you sow, the more you reap" (2 Co 9, 6), impressed him deeply. He was a **zealous sower of God's word.** *He sowed it abundantly and was privileged to reap abundantly, founding on 8 September 1875, the Divine Word Missionaries in Steyl.*

Goch on the Lower Rhine

Arnold Janssen,
1890

6

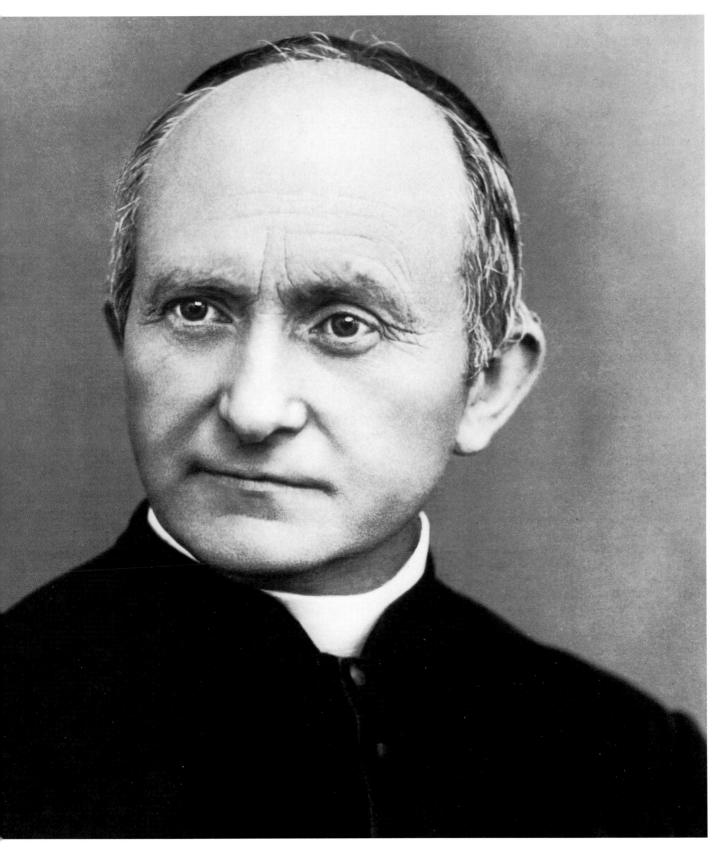

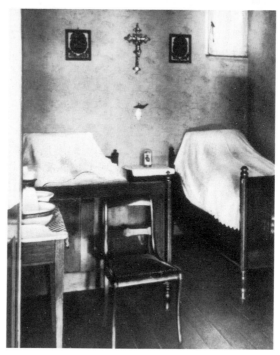

Room in which
Arnold Janssen
was born

**Birthplace
of Arnold Janssen
in Goch**

1. Home and Family

*The house in which Arnold Janssen was born still
stands today in Frauenstrasse, Goch. In a small room
he first saw the light of day.*

1837.
Novembris.
5. Maria Huberta Ebben
nata, filia legitima W...
Adolphi Ebben ac Fr...
Aerssen, baptizata est a...
Pastore, de S. fonte Antoni...
Huberto Ebben ac Petro...
Hendriks, nata Ebben, ...

6ta Arnoldus Janssen, heri ho...
natus, filius legitimus ...
gen & Catharinae Well...
tus est a me J. A. Leci...
S. fonte enim Arnoldo...
& Maria op gen Hoff...

His parents were ordinary citizens of Goch. His father, Gerhard Johann Janssen, was in the transportation business.

My **father** was a plain and simple man, a concerned father and a good Christian. On Sundays he would faithfully attend Mass, going to church twice in the morning and once again in the afternoon. He regularly attended Mass every Monday, and on other days when possible, to ask the Holy Spirit for guidance in the week's activities. He insisted that his family partake frequently of the Sacraments of Reconciliation and the Eucharist and that his children lead responsible Christian lives. . . .

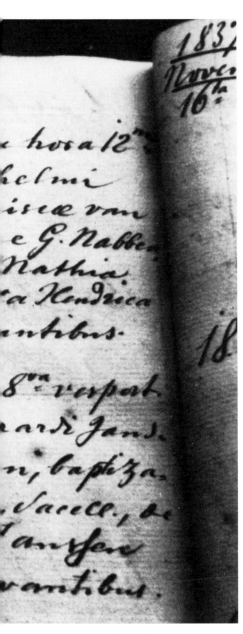

Baptismal Register of 1837

Baptismal Font of the Parish Church in Goch; now in the Arnold Janssen Church in Goch

He owned small parcels of land and rented other farm land which he cultivated. He had two horses, since in addition to his agricultural activities, he operated a transport business making weekly trips to Nymwegen to deliver and bring back merchandise. He also drove regularly to Geldern and Straelen to fetch salt. Upon his return from these trips, Mother would send us children out to meet him.

On the occasion of his father's birthday, 28 December 1854, the 16-year-old Arnold Janssen wrote:

Dear Father,

Today is your birthday, a joyful and festive day for you because 53 years ago you saw the light of day. It is no less joyful for us. If you celebrate this day in honor of the One who gave you life, so too do we celebrate it as the day that He gave us the one to whom we owe our very existence. He conferred upon us, dear Father, the greatest benefactor we have on earth. Immeasurably great and manifold are the gifts we received from you.

St. Mary Magdalen Parish Church, Goch

We cannot even count all the wonderful things you do for us; the many expressions of your kindness and love for us. Each day brings new instances. Still less can we repay you for all you have accomplished for us. This can only be achieved by Him who dwells above – Almighty God. May He, the God of justice, who rewards the giving of even a cup of water in His name, repay you a thousandfold for what you have done for us. This ought to be the thrust of our prayer each day.

We want to do all that we can. We want to repay your love with our own, and if in the past we have not always shown loyal and ready obedience – for which we now beg your pardon – we shall try to bring you joy in the future through our constant diligence and prompt obedience. This we promise on this festive occasion.

His mother, Anna Katharina Janssen, nee Wellesen, was born in Weeze near Goch. At the age of 60, Arnold Janssen recalls:

My **mother,** a good woman, who even before her marriage suffered much from digestive disorders, was to experience many heartaches and hard work in her married life. God blessed her with many children, and in addition to her domestic chores, she also looked after the animals, including four cows and a number of pigs. There was but one woman servant to assist her.

She was a great lover of prayer. This was manifest particularly in her widowhood when my brother and his young wife joined our household. This freed my elderly mother to devote more time to prayer and to attend as many Masses as possible in our church, frequently remaining in prayer until 9 o'clock, long after the last Mass had ended. Sometimes she would return home between Masses but would then remain even longer in church afterwards.

If there were a late service, she invariably would be one of the first to arrive and the last to leave. . . . She spent practically all of Sunday in church, from early morning until 11:30 with only a brief interruption for breakfast and then again in the afternoon from 2 or 2:30 until 4 or 5 o'clock. Even in her old age she continued to wear the same simple style of clothing she had worn in her youth.

"She was a praying mother in the fullest sense of the word," *commented one of Arnold Janssen's brothers, Capuchin Brother Juniperus.*

**Chair in which
Arnold Janssen's mother
died in 1891**

Original tombstone of the Janssen family in Goch

On 25 November 1856, his mother's name day, Arnold Janssen, a seminarian in Münster, wrote:

My dearly beloved Mother,

Today on your name day, beloved Mother, I am moved to send you a few words from afar to convey my warmest wishes and to express these sentiments which I desire to share with you.

Before anything else, dear Mother, my heartfelt best wishes on your feast day which you celebrate today. This feast which commemorates the patron saint of your baptism, the devout and learned St. Katharina, must certainly call to mind your own baptism and the joyous days of your innocent childhood. I too am reminded of my childhood and of the one who stood by my cradle, looking upon her young charge with a mother's loving eye, watching over him, caring and praying for him, nursing him with her milk, and nourishing his soul with the still better milk of sound teaching and exhortation to love God and neighbor. As I think of these things, my soul is stirred and my loving wishes become even more fervent. More ardent too is my heart's yearning to recommend you, dear Mother, to God, the Lord of all, and to implore His grace and blessing upon you.

Arnold Janssen with four of his brothers left to right: Theodor, Peter, Wilhelm (Brother Juniperus OFM Cap), Gerhard, St. Wendel 1904

"I thank God that none of my brothers and sisters have ever caused me any sorrow," *commented Arnold Janssen at the age of 62. Johannes, the youngest of his eight brothers and sisters, joined the Divine Word Missionaries in Steyl and was ordained priest in 1876.*

Wilhelm, the third-youngest brother, joined the Capuchins in Münster as Brother Juniperus. On that occasion, 12 November 1863, Arnold Janssen wrote his father:

First of all I wish to thank you for so promptly sharing with me the news of Wilhelm's decision, one that concerns us all so intimately. I must confess that it is a long time since anything has brought me as much joy as did this news. The call to the monastic life is a great blessing indeed. The more I am convinced that I do not have such a calling, the more I envy those who are chosen by a loving God to serve Him exclusively in the quiet of a monastic cell. It is true, as Wilhelm says, that compared with loving and serving God, all else in the world is vanity. When this short life span is over, this will become frightfully clear to us. It would be a dreadful obstinacy if one were clearly to hear God's call to the monastic life and refuse to follow the gentle voice of the Holy Spirit. It is a great blessing for Wilhelm and a sign of God's love for our whole family. If you have not yet thanked God for it, please do so soon and offer tonight's rosary in gratitude.

Pulpit in Parish
Church in Goch

Desk with Jansse
family's bool
"Lives of th
Saints,
Rosary o
Brother Juniper⸱
Janssen (made ⸱
cherry seed⸱

Concerning their religious upbringing at home, Brother Juniperus (Wilhelm Janssen) had this to say:

"Our father ruled our home as a patriarch. Our conversation at meals on Sundays and Holy Days revolved around the sermon message and he would question the servants and us children on it. At the conclusion of the meal we had to remain seated while Father, bareheaded, read the entire Gospel and the accompanying explanation from **Goffine's Handbook.** Then, he took the catechism, and each child, in chronological order, was required to recite verbatim all the questions and answers of the catechism lesson (he had) assigned the previous Sunday. We were not permitted to leave the house until we were able to respond fluently and accurately. Then Father would put his hand in his vest pocket and give each of us two Pfennige."

**Library of
the Augustinian College,
Gaesdonck**

2. Student and Seminarian

*Father Ruiter, the associate pastor, played a decisive
role in Arnold Janssen's life:*

"Without the help of Father Ruiter, Arnold
would have had to do the ploughing at home as
did the rest of us. He would never have
become a priest," *noted one of his brothers.*

Arnold himself relates:

Many processions passed through Goch on their
way to Kevelaer, and since I had become an
altarboy at a very early age I was able to serve for
benediction on these occasions.

I usually served Mass daily for an elderly priest, Father Lax, whom I had to fetch at his house each morning. Father Nabben, the parish priest at Goch, was a tall and robust Dutchman who preached in Dutch, whereas his associates preached in German.

Church life in Goch was quite good. The sacristan was Mister Lueben whose family could boast of two priests and two religious. They were an exemplary family and were considered as very pious and religious by the townspeople. Father Ruiter, a zealous and quite severe man, also had a strong influence on me through his piety and simple lifestyle. He had an excellent library of religious books, and when I went to him for religious instruction he would lend me books on the lives of the saints, for example, the life of Joseph of Cupertino. When I was ten years old, a middle school was opened in Goch with Father Gemès, a religious, as its principal. Father Ruiter immediately visited my parents and persuaded them to send me there. Without his help it is quite likely that I would not have been able to attend school since my parents considered our family too poor to permit me to take up further studies. But Father Ruiter convinced them to do so and rely on Divine Providence.

Arnold Janssen recalls the beginning of his secondary education:

It was a great joy for me when I started my studies. I recall vividly that very morning of 2 January when we had our first class in a small private house in Frauentor. Studying did not come easy to me. Although my grades were good, my knowledge remained very limited.

A year and a half later, a diocesan minor seminary, the Augustinian College, was opened in the old Augustinian Monastery of Gaesdonck, about three kilometers from Goch. Arnold Janssen immediately applied for admission and studied there until he began his philosophical-theological studies.

Wilhelm van Gülk, our neighbor, Johann Janssen, a distant relative and I were the three students from Goch who applied for admission to Gaesdonck. Admission exams were set for the second Monday in September; 54 candidates applied. All were required to write a German composition and complete a German-Latin exercise. We were also examined in Latin-German translations, mathematics, religion and Bible History. For the last two subjects, the examiner was the dean of the cathedral, Doctor Krabbe. He was a simple man and was highly regarded for establishing the Augustinian College. Later, he served as Diocesan Commissioner and came every August to give the final exams. . . .

We had to return the following Tuesday when, about noon, the results were announced to us. What joy when I heard my name among the 24 successful candidates. Since then I have often wondered how I managed to pass the exams as my neighbor Gülk was a much better informed student than I. I had studied Latin, the main subject, for only a year and a half and had not yet reached the third level, which was hardly possible after only one and a half years of study. This soon became evident once classes began and I produced the poorest composition. Both my cousin and I were told that we must take additional private lessons in Latin. . . . Upon learning that I had been admitted, I hurried to tell the good news to my parents who were visiting my uncle at the parish fair in Gocherheide. . . .

We entered Gaesdonck in mid-October and the following day a solemn High Mass was celebrated to commemorate the opening of the College. Doctor Perger, the rector, preached the sermon. What an impression this celebration made upon me! Only later did I fully realize to what extent I should thank God for putting me at such an early age under the protection and guidance of Holy Church.

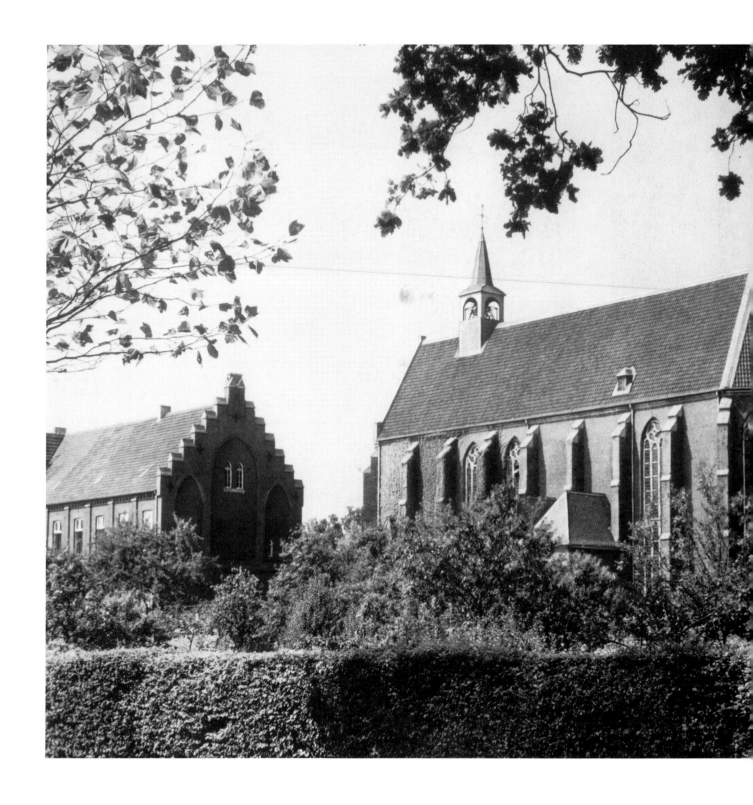

**Church and Refectory,
Augustinian College,
Gaesdonck**

Doctor Clemens Perger was the first rector of the Augustinian College. For 25 years, until the compulsory closing of the school during the cultural revolution of Bismarck, he directed the formation of the 771 students who attended the school. Arnold Janssen maintained a close friendship with him throughout his entire life. Doctor Perger, who later became the dean of the Cathedral in Münster, outlived his former pupil by more than a year. He died on 11 June 1910 at the age of 94. His body rests in the cathedral cemetery in Münster.

Father Clemens Perger, Rector at Gaesdonck from 1849 to 1873

Doctor Perger took great pains to give us a good education. He was a man of outstanding talent and an excellent teacher, especially in mathematics. Every evening after night prayers, he conducted a spiritual conference. The six Aloysian Sundays were observed each year, and the May devotions were celebrated with great solemnity. I am deeply indebted to the Augustinian College for the inspiration it gave me.

In the summer of 1850 or 1851, the Bishop was scheduled to visit the Augustinian College and to administer the Sacrament of Confirmation to all who had not yet been confirmed. There were only two of us: a student named Berchen and I. After the evening conference, Father Rector called us to his office and strongly counselled us to prepare ourselves well for the reception of this Sacrament. If I recall correctly, he also suggested that we pay a special visit to the Blessed Sacrament each day; this we did, sometimes even twice a day. I took the preparation very seriously. In retrospect, I have the firm conviction that had I not done so I would not have received the graces God bestowed upon me in my later life. I must always be grateful to Doctor Perger for his excellent advice and guidance.

CONSOLATRIX AFFLICTORVM ORA PRO NOBIS

Vera Effigies Matris IESU Consolatricis afflicto-
rum in agro suburbano Lvxemburgi Miraculis
et Hominum Visitatione celebris, Anno 1640.

**Picture and Chapel
of Our Lady,
Consoler of the Afflicted,
Kevelaer**

Each year during the autumn vacation, Arnold with one of his brothers would make a pilgrimage to Kevelaer, a distance of about eight kilometers. Brother Juniperus reports:

"It was probably in 1858 when, early one Sunday morning, we made a pilgrimage to Kevelaer. Arnold led in prayer. We began right at our gate and continued throughout the two-hour walk to Kevelaer. There we went to confession, and after receiving Holy Communion and making a long thanksgiving, we left the so-called large candle chapel which was filled with pilgrims from all over. 'Wilhelm,' Arnold said to me, 'you must be as hungry as I am, but, Wilhelm, we don't want to go to a restaurant. Here are two Groschen for **Apfeltarten.' Apfeltarten** or apple tart was a pastry made of a thin piece of dough covered with thin slices of apple and baked in the oven.

"By now it must have been almost 11 AM. Arnold enthusiastically praised the apple tart, his favorite dessert. Then we resumed our devotions and returned home praying all the way."

27

In October 1855 Arnold Janssen began his philosoph-
ical and theological studies at Münster's Borromeo
College, which had been established only one year
earlier. At the same time, he also attended the
lectures of Professor Hels and Professor Hittorf on
mathematics and physics and of Professor Karsch
on botany and zoology at the Royal Prussian
Theological and Philosophical Academy.

Borromeo College,
Münster,
at the time
of Arnold Janssen

Arnold Janssen was only nineteen and a half when he completed his studies in philosophy, still almost three years too young to enter the major seminary. Hence, heeding the Bishop's recommendation to all candidates interested in the teaching profession, he went to the University of Bonn to study for his state examination as a middle school teacher.

Together with his old Gaesdonck classmate, Lambert Lamers, Janssen began his studies in Bonn. Lamers later became the director of the State Civil School of Hertogenbosch.

I joined the Sodality of the Blessed Virgin in Bonn, as I had in Münster. I was happy when my fellow classmate Lambert Lamers, an old Gaesdoncker, joined me in Bonn in the autumn of 1857. We became close friends during those years of study, attending Mass together every morning and receiving the Sacraments every fortnight. We also observed the six Aloysian Sundays in the Sodality. Father Voiss was our director. When we did not do our own cooking, we lunched at Badenheuer's.

To prepare for the final exam I had to study most diligently as the exams covered the entire scientific field, including history and a number of other subjects. Thank God, I passed the exam successfully.

The Cathedral
of Münster,
about 1800

Notation
of Arnold Janssen's
Diaconate,
Ordination Register
of the Diocese
of Münster

After his success in the state teachers' exam in Bonn in 1859, Arnold Janssen was offered but declined a teaching position in Berlin with a yearly salary of 800 Taler – a very tempting offer for a young man of 22. Instead, he returned to Münster to begin his theological studies. In August 1860 he passed the Seminary exams and began his final preparation for the priesthood.

Münster Cathedral

**List of Lectures,
"Münster Anzeiger",
1859**

A letter to his mother on the occasion of her name day, nine months before his ordination, gives us an insight into the young theologian's world of thought:

I am sitting here all alone in my small room in the early dawn. Next to me the candle is still burning; in front of me is a picture of Christ. All is quiet and peaceful, and there is great peace in my soul. From a church steeple, near or far away, I can hear the sound of a bell chiming through the dark night, calling the faithful to rise from sleep and come to church where the Holy Sacrifice of the Mass is being prepared. I am deeply moved as I reflect: you too will soon go to the altar, and in the place of Christ celebrate that sacred mystery. Then my thoughts return to this peaceful and tranquil place where I have been preparing myself for the past few days for that holy act. I think back over the years that have elapsed: the days of my early childhood, of growing up in my parents' home, of the happy hours when I realized that you would consent to my heart's desire for further study; then, the long student years come alive again with their efforts, struggles, and dangers. And now,

after having happily entered the seminary, I am about to be ordained and perhaps within a year be active in my pastoral ministry.

When I seriously reflect on all this, I realize how deeply I am indebted to God for his paternal guidance. He has given me success in everything, he has protected me from illness and disturbing misfortunes, while many of my classmates are either sickly or have already died before achieving the goal of their many years of study. It was his providential hand which kept me from falling into scholastic pitfalls. To whom must I give credit for all this? The image of my dear mother comes before me: how she nursed and cared for me in my childhood and guided me along the right path. She never ceased praying for me daily even when I was far away from home, constantly imploring the Giver of all good things to bestow His blessings upon me.

33

Janssen was ordained Subdeacon on 16 March and Deacon on 25 May. On 7 August 1861, one week before his ordination, he wrote:

Dear Parents,

What you have longed for for so many years will soon be accomplished.

After passing my written exams on 27 and 28 July, I and five other seminarians were examined orally by the Vicar General. The retreat will begin tonight; Ordination will take place on Thursday, 15 August. On that day the Lord will number me among his priests. Two days later (Saturday, the 17th) I will, God willing, have for the first time the extraordinary privilege of offering to the Lord the Sacrifice of His Son, our Savior.

Rejoice with me and praise the Lord who has guided my steps so lovingly and now wills to do this great thing to me. In the coming days He will manifest His infinite goodness to me in an even greater measure. Please pray fervently for me and offer your daily work for me so that the Lord may grant that I may never become an unworthy priest in His ministry. In His immense goodness, He has perhaps already stretched out His hands to bestow great blessings upon my Ordination, or perhaps He is waiting for you to ask Him to grant me such blessings. Please do ask; ask most fervently. The Lord will provide the means with which I shall be able to repay you abundantly. I shall remember you in my first Holy Mass.

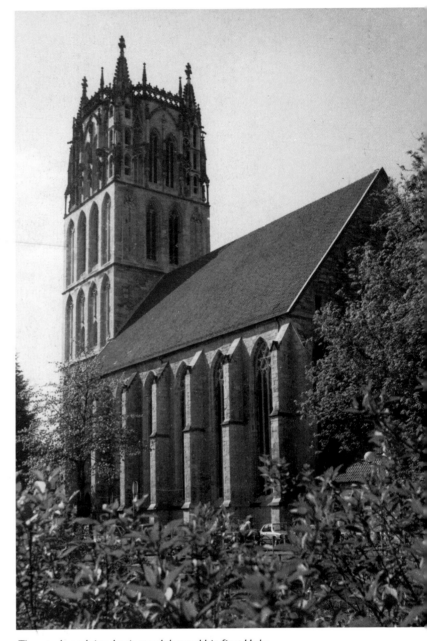

The newly ordained priest celebrated his first Holy Mass at the main altar in the Liebfrauen church in Münster, the oldest Marian church in the diocese. Doctor Giese, the prefect of the theologians and future Vicar General, assisted him. His fellow students, van Bebber and Bless, served the Mass. His father was kneeling in the nave of the church.

In the first reading for that day we find the words: "Do not forget: thin sowing means thin reaping; the more you sow, the more you reap" (2 Co 9, 6) and in the Gospel: "Unless a wheat grain falls on the ground and dies, it remains only a single grain; but if it dies, it yields a rich harvest" (Jn 12, 24).

These words made a deep impression on me. My good father had come to Münster for the ceremony. He was present at my first Mass and, if I am not mistaken, also at my Ordination. It was only in the beginning of September that I went home to celebrate my first Holy Mass there in all the routine calm of a normal workday. At that time, there were no public celebrations on such occasions.

Pastor Wellesen, uncle of Mrs. Janssen, mother of the Founder of Steyl, d. 1876 (Portrait in the Rectory, Kaldenkirchen)

Kaldenkirchen Parish Church

The newly ordained priest preached his first sermon on 8 September 1861 in Kaldenkirchen where his mother's uncle was pastor. He chose as the theme for his sermon: "The Archconfraternity of the Most Holy and Immaculate Heart of Mary for the Conversion of Sinners."

36

3. Priest and Teacher

It was more than a month later when Arnold Janssen began his work as middle school teacher at the Secondary School in Bocholt.

Bocholt was a large and flourishing parish with 5,000 urban parishioners and a rural population of 4,000. The pastor was Father Tarnhorst, a native of Münster and an able man. There were also nine or ten other priests residing in the rectory, many of whom took their noon and evening meals there as payment for their services.

I normally taught 24 hours a week, a number which rose to 30 during the war years of 1870 and 1871 when we were obliged to take over the classes of a drafted colleague. In addition, I had four to six assignments to correct each week. This added a considerable amount of work, especially the corrections in mathematics which can be very tedious if done properly. Overall, my stay in Bocholt was most instructive. The priests and in particular the religious zeal of the Catholics inspired me immensely. Little by little, I was called upon to teach all first level subjects. Eventually, with the growing number of pupils and teachers, I concentrated solely on teaching mathematics, business accounting, natural sciences and French.

Arnold Janssen further comments on his years in Bocholt, where he stayed until 1873:

During those years the parish church was completely restored with the efficient help of the entire clergy. The beautiful divine services were particularly edifying for me and made me aware how important it is for a Catholic community that divine services be properly planned and celebrated with due solemnity. During the Easter Season, Matins were said each Sunday, and I attended whenever I could. Frequently I was asked to assist at the services, but always as Subdeacon. I never sang a High Mass in Bocholt, because when I did so in Dingden, it created so much comment that I gave up the experiment and never tried it a second time. In general, the years spent in Bocholt were happy and active ones.

First Secondary School in Bocholt where Arnold Janssen lived and taught from 1861–1867 (today, the Parish Rectory of Liebfrauen)

Rector Waldau, Director of the Secondary School, gave the following appraisal of Arnold Janssen's work in Bocholt:

"Arnold Janssen, born in Goch on 5 November 1837, has been employed in this school since 15 October 1861. In April 1862 he was appointed temporary teacher and in November 1863 as first permanent teacher. He worked in that capacity until the fall of 1873 when he resigned.

"During that time, he taught middle and secondary school subjects with special emphasis on mathematics and the natural sciences. All mathematics and natural science courses on the second level were entrusted to him. He was also chosen as class sponsor for all classes with the exception of the second level. His teaching showed that he had thoroughly and fully mastered his subject matter. He prepared himself carefully for each lesson and took great pains to present the matter as clearly as possible. He taught his pupils to give precise answers by phrasing his questions in plain language. He knew how to get his students to study hard for their classes. He corrected the written compositions with great conscientiousness. The results he achieved deserve full recognition. He worked equally hard in securing the necessary instruments for the physics department and in the collection of scientific specimens.

"He was a firm disciplinarian in the classroom. Both in and outside the classroom, he zealously tried to encourage and strengthen his pupils to lead good moral and religious lives.

"He fostered a good relationship with his fellow teachers, and his private life won the general respect of all. The school saw him leave with great regret."

*In 1867, Arnold Janssen went to Innsbruck to attend
the General Convention of the Catholic Organizations
in Germany and Austria. It played a decisive role in his
spiritual development.*

When the General Convention of the Catholic
Organizations of Germany and Austria met in
Innsbruck in 1867, I extended my holidays in order
to attend. There I became acquainted with Father
Malfatti, S.J., Director of the Apostleship of Prayer
in Germany and Austria. He asked me to become
the promoter of that organization in the diocese of
Münster. I agreed to do so.

In the fall of the same year, I also visited the grave
of the saintly Cure of Ars on my way to the
industrial exhibition in Paris. After that, I gave my
full attention to the Apostleship of Prayer. What
appealed to me in particular was the offering of
one's daily work for the intentions of the Heart of
Jesus. After 1867 all my holidays were spent
faithfully promoting the Apostleship of Prayer in
the diocese of Münster. Formally appointed its
Diocesan Director in 1869, I sought to develop the
spirit of intercession and to encourage the offering
of daily prayer, such as the Rosary, for the
intentions of the Sacred Heart. Toward that end, I
composed five intentions for the recitation of the
Rosary. They were widely circulated. Many church-
es adopted them and they were frequently incor-
porated into the school Mass.

I succeeded in introducing the Apostleship of
Prayer in practically the entire diocese of Münster;

there were only a few pastors whom I did not visit for this purpose.

In order to serve the Church even better, Father Janssen resigned his Bocholt position in the fall of 1873 and became the chaplain for the Ursuline Sisters in Kempen.

While in Bocholt, my desire grew to contribute more to the spiritual advancement of the Church, especially in the foreign missions. But my many activities and in particular the nature of the subjects I taught (natural sciences, physics, mathematics and French) left me with little possibility for further initiatives in this field. I yearned to assume a position where I could develop my ideas, even though it meant resigning my position in Bocholt. I wanted to be free to publish a popular monthly magazine for the promotion of prayer and participation in the great intentions of our Divine Savior, particularly the spreading of the faith. I finally told my director and colleagues that I wanted to resign my position in Bocholt. I went to Münster to share and discuss my ideas with Bishop J.B. Brinkmann. I traveled by foot and on the way I made a number of stops to promote the Apostleship of Prayer. I arrived in Münster on 23 February 1873 and on the following day was received by the Bishop. He gave me a cordial welcome and to my great surprise immediately gave me permission to resign from Bocholt. This I did without delay. Until then my project had been considered an idle dream by all with whom I had discussed it. The reaction was one of a tolerant indifference. They told me later that they didn't even try to talk me out of it because they felt that the Bishop would be clever and intelligent enough to immediately see the foolishness of my ideas and not give me permission to resign.

During the autumn holidays of 1873, Arnold Janssen made great efforts to arrange to have a daily Mass offered for Christian Unity at the tomb of St. Boniface, the Apostle of Germany, in the Cathedral of Fulda.

In October 1873, he took up his chaplaincy at the Ursuline Convent.

Pietà,
Chapel of
Ursuline Sisters,
Kempen

1874, Nr. 1. Erſter Jahrgang.　　　Paderborn, Januar 1874.

Kleiner Herz = Jeſu-Bote

Mit kirchlicher Approbation.

Gebet des Leſers beim Beginn der Leſung.

Herr Jeſu Chriſte. Ich bete Dich an als den Sohn Gottes, und durch die Vermittlung Deiner ſüßeſten Mutter flehe ich zu Dir. Sende mir die Gnade des h. Geiſtes aus der Fülle Deines liebenden Herzens, auf daß Er mich Unwiſſenden erleuchte, mich Sündenbefleckten reinige und heilige und mich in Deiner h. Liebe befeſtige. Amen. Darum flehe ich zu Dir durch die Liebe des Vaters und des h. Geiſtes, durch die Fülle Deiner unendlichen Barmherzigkeit und durch die Verdienſte aller Deiner Heiligen. Amen.

1. Lied zum göttlichen Kinde Jeſu.

Liebſter Jeſu in der Krippe,
Liebſter Jeſu, göttlich Kind!
Mach' mein Herz zu Deiner Krippe,
Daß ich Deine Liebe find'.

Liebſter Jeſu in dem Stalle,
Liebſter Jeſu, göttlich Kind!
Hilf' und rett' und heil' uns Alle,
Daß ein Jeder werd' Dein Kind.

Liebſter Jeſu in den Windeln,
Liebſter Jeſu, göttlich Kind!
Bind' uns Alle mit den Windeln
Deiner Liebe ſüß und lind.

2. Die h. Mutter Anna.

Feſt: Am 26. Juli.

(Nach den Mittheilungen der gottſeligen Catharina Emmerich, geboren 1774 bei Coesfeld in Weſtfalen in einem Hauſe ohne Rauchfang. Schon als Kind von 4–5 Jahren unermüdliche nächtliche Beterin, 1802 Auguſtinerin auf dem Agnetenberg bei Dülmen. 1812 mit den hh. fünf Wunden geſchmückt, und von da an ohne Speiſe lebend, faſt beſtändig dem Tode nahe. Mit Jeſu gekreuzigt. Gegenſtand des Widerſpruchs und feindſeliger Unterſuchung. Eine faſt ununterbrochen wachende, betende, helfende, nimmer müde Arbeiterin im Weinberge des Herrn. Die große Prophetin des 19. Jahrhunderts und aller vorangegangenen Jahrhunderte. Beſtimmt, vieles Alte neu zu wecken, bei Vielen das Leben im Glauben zu ſtärken. † zu Dülmen 1824 den 9. Februar.)

„Die hl. Mutter Anna ſtammte väterlicher Seits aus Levi, mütterlicher Seits aus Benjamin. Ich ſah in einer Betrachtung die Bundeslade von ihren Vorfahren ſo fromm und andächtig tragen, und daß ſie damals Strahlen des Segens aus ihr empfingen, welche ſich auf ihre Nachkommenſchaft Anna und Maria, bezogen." (Leben Mariä Seite 58.)

„Die Eltern der h. Anna waren reich. Ich ſah dies an ihrer großen Wirthſchaft. Sie hatten viele Ochſen. Aber ſie hatten nichts für ſich allein. Sie gaben Alles den Armen. Ich habe die h. Anna als Kind geſehen. Sie war nicht beſonders ſchön, aber doch ſchöner als Andre. So ſchön als Maria war ſie bei weitem nicht, aber ungemein einfältig,

kindlich und fromm. So habe ich ſie allezeit geſehen, auch als Jungfrau, als Mutter und als altes Mütterchen, ſo daß, wenn ich eine recht kindliche alte Bauersfrau ſah, ich immer denken mußte: die iſt wie Anna. Sie hatte noch mehrere Geſchwiſter, Brüder und Schweſtern (z. B. Sobe, Maraha.) Dieſelben wurden verheirathet. Sie aber wollte noch nicht heirathen. Ihre Eltern hatten ſie beſonders lieb. Sie hatte wohl an ſechs Freier; aber ſie ſchlug ſie aus." (L. M. S. 20.)

Da ſie aber wie ihre Vorfahren ſich bei den frommen Einſiedlern des Berges Horeb Rath erholte, empfing ſie von dieſen durch Eingebung Gottes die Weiſung, den h. Joachim zu heirathen. Dieſen kannte ſie damals noch nicht. Als ihr Vater Eliud aber in das Thal Zabulon zog, wo Joachims Vater Matthat wohnte, bewarb er ſich um ſie.

„Joachim und Anna wurden an einem kleinen Orte getraut, wo nur eine geringe Schule war. Anna war etwa 19 Jahre alt. Sie hatten Beide etwas Ausgezeichnetes in ihrem Weſen. Sie waren zwar ganz jüdiſch. Aber es war etwas in ihnen, was ſie ſelbſt nicht kannten, ein wunderbarer Ernſt. Ich habe ſie ſelten lachen ſehen, wenn ſie gleich im Anfang ihrer Ehe nicht eigentlich traurig waren. Sie hatten einen ſtillen, gleichmäßigen Charakter, und in ihrem friſchen Alter ſchon etwas von alten geſetzten Leuten. Ich habe wohl in meiner Jugend ſchon ſolche junge Paare geſehen, die ſehr geſetzt waren, und bei denen ich damals ſchon dachte: die ſind gerade wie die hh. Anna und Joachim."

„Der h. Joachim war arm. Aber die Eltern der h. Anna waren wohlhabend. Sie hatten viele Heerden, ſchöne Teppiche und Geſchirre und viele Knechte und Mägde. Den Acker habe ich ſie nie bauen ſehen, wohl aber Vieh treiben auf die Weide. Sie waren ſehr fromm, innig, wohlthätig, ſchlicht und recht. Sie theilten oft ihre Heerden und Alles in drei Theile. Ein Drittel des Viehes gaben ſie in den Tempel, und das trieben ſie ſelbſt hin, wo es von den Tempeldienern empfangen wurde. Das zweite Drittel gaben ſie den Armen oder an begehrende Anverwandten, deren meiſtens Einige zugegen waren, die es wegtrieben. Das letzte und gewöhnlich geringſte Drittel behielten ſie für ſich. Sie lebten ſehr mäßig und gaben Alles hin, wo begehrt ward. Da hab' ich oft ſchon als Kind gedacht: „Geben reicht aus; wer gibt, erhält doppelt wieder." Denn ich ſah, daß ihr Drittel ſich immer wieder mehrte, ſo daß Alles bald wieder ſo vollauf war, daß ſie wieder in drei Theile theilen konnten."

„Sie hatten viele Verwandte, die bei allen feierlichen Gelegenheiten bei ihnen verſammelt waren. Da ſah ich dann nie viel Schmauſerei. Ich ſah ſie wohl in ihrem Leben hie und da einem Armen Speiſe reichen. Aber eigentliche Gaſtmahle ſah ich nie. Wenn ſie zuſammen waren, ſah ich ſie gewöhnlich im Kreis an der Erde liegen, und von Gott mit einer allmälig ergänzen und uns Ihren göttlichen Segen nicht vorenthalten.

Kempen bei Crefeld, am Feste des süßen Namens Jesu 1874.

Der Redacteur.

Nun noch ein Wort über die Tendenz unserer Zeitschrift. Der Haupt=, wenn auch nicht alleinige Zweck derselben ist, über die katholischen Missionen des In= und Auslandes auf faßliche und anregende Weise zu belehren. Neben uns arbeiten zu demselben Zwecke, aber mehr für die gebildeten Stände, „die katholischen Missionen". Wir wünschen dieser Zeitschrift Gedeihen und Vermehrung ihres zahlreichen Leserkreises und empfehlen sie zu dem Ende hiermit. Sie und wir arbeiten selbstständig zu demselben Zwecke, aber auf verschiedene Weise. Deshalb werden die meisten Leser Beides, zusammen mit Nutzen und Interesse lesen. — Dies zum Beweise unserer Gesinnung gegen die trefflichen Männer, welche „die katholischen Missionen" herausgeben und verlegen. Die Gründe, weshalb wir das Erscheinen unserer Zeitschrift neben den Genannten für nützlich gehalten haben, sind an einer andern Stelle bereits öffentlich angegeben. Sie liegen für den, der Beides kennt, sehr nahe. Der Obige.

Redacteur: **Arnold Janssen.**
Druck und Commissions=Verlag der **Bonifacius=Druckerei in Paderborn.**
(P. Kleine.)

A final word on the aim of the publication: i.e. to report principally on the home and foreign missions

As early as January 1874, Arnold Janssen published the first issue of the **Little Messenger of the Sacred Heart,** *a magazine which served as a vehicle for his ideas. Later, it became one of the main sources of help in the founding of a mission seminary. It was printed in Paderborn; Arnold Janssen personally took care of the editing, publishing and distribution. In 1903, the magazine was renamed the* **Steyl Mission Messenger** *and continued publication until silenced by the National Socialist Party in 1941.*

The title, **Little Messenger of the Sacred Heart,** alludes to its role as emissary for the desires of the Sacred Heart of Jesus. The **Little Messenger of the Sacred Heart** aims primarily to arouse interest in the Catholic Church's foreign mission among pagans. . . . A religious writer has said that the highest and most deserving of all deeds is the salvation of souls. This is crystal clear because this was the very mission of Jesus himself. He who spreads the faith or contributes to its increase saves not just one soul but the souls of many when we consider not only the converts themselves but also their descendants.

Our magazine is devoted to this great work. We hope to win more prayer and sacrifice for Him. We hope to revive, here and there, a dormant missionary vocation.

We also hope to inspire many Catholic mothers to beg God for the blessing of a missionary son.

Finally we hope that the reports of the heroic and virtuous endeavors of missionaries and their companions may serve as the catalyst to stir us out of the lethargy which so characterizes our generation and prompt us to action concerning this religious priority.

In an article in the June issue of the **Little Messenger of the Sacred Heart** *under the heading, "Various Requests to Various People, Submitted in the Name of the Most Sacred Heart of Jesus," Arnold Janssen asked both priests and seminarians, especially those on the threshold of the priesthood:*

Is there not one among you in the whole of Germany who feels called to devote himself to the missionary cause?

What would happen if German priests were to work together to organize a German mission seminary in a safe place? Such a venture, as this writer knows for certain, is in line with the wishes of the Propagation of the Faith in Rome, and even more so, with the express wish of the Holy Father himself.

Belgium, Ireland, Italy and France all have mission seminaries. There are four in Italy and five in Paris; yet Germany, this large country with so many devout Catholic families, does not have even one unless we consider North America as a mission country and look upon the American College in Münster as a mission seminary. We believe that something can and should be done about it. We would be prepared, in as far as we can do so, to arrange a meeting of like-minded persons.

These thoughts were the first steps towards the foundation of the future Steyl. After much hesitation and prayer, Janssen finally decided to translate his dream into reality. He was further encouraged by Bishop Raimondi, the Vicar Apostolic of Hong Kong, who very bluntly and clearly responded to his repeated complaint about the lack of a German mission seminary with the challenge "Found one yourself." *He further confirmed this challenge by personally visiting Janssen in Kempen. On this occasion, the Bishop also advised him to contact Doctor Ludwig von Essen, the parish priest of Neuwerk near Mönchengladbach, who was also interested and making efforts toward the realization of a mission seminary.*

In May 1874 I read in the **Gladbacher Volkszeitung** that Bishop Raimondi was visiting Doctor von Essen in Neuwerk. I went to see the Bishop there to learn more about the missions in order that I might better awaken and promote interest in them through the **Little Messenger of the Sacred Heart.** I again expressed my regret that Germany had no seminary of its own for the training of missionaries. They existed in France, Italy, Belgium and even England, a country where, unlike Germany, Catholicism is not as flourishing. I further explained to the Bishop that I myself was too old to go to the missions. "But this is not necessary," replied Bishop Raimondi, "it is also important that there remain priests in the homeland, here in Germany, who will dedicate themselves to this purpose."

I went to see Bishop Raimondi a second time. Finally, the Bishop said that if there were no other German priests to join me in establishing a mission seminary, then I should found the seminary myself with complete trust in Divine Providence, and for this purpose I should contact Doctor von Essen. The idea of founding a mission seminary myself had never occurred to me, and I quickly dismissed the whole idea. I felt that I was not capable of such an endeavor. Later, Bishop Raimondi visited me in Kempen and even more insistently urged me to take up the task. As in the past, I refused. I still hoped to arouse interest in a mission seminary by bringing the idea to the public through the **Little Messenger of the Sacred Heart.**

Although several appeals were subsequently published in the **Little Messenger of the Sacred Heart,** *they elicited not a single response. Doctor von Essen, though interested, was not free to leave his parish because of Bismarck's cultural revolutionary laws. Had he left, he could not have been replaced. Hence, Arnold Janssen was forced to concede that it was up to him to establish a mission seminary.*

The same cultural revolutionary laws prohibited the foundation of the mission seminary on German soil. Therefore, Janssen's gaze crossed the border of Germany into neighboring Holland.

Arnold Janssen,
about 1886

**Bishop Raimondi,
1827–1894,
Apostolic Vicar
of Hong Kong**

**Bishop
Josef Augustinus Paredis,
Roermond, d. 1886**

**Bishop
Johann Bernhard Brinkmann,
Münster, d. 1889**

4. A Mission Seminary in Steyl

*Arnold Janssen first found a tract of land in Tegelen,
Netherlands. After long negotiations, he could have
bought it for 45,000 Marks. The Bishop of Roermond, in whose diocese Tegelen is situated, gave his
consent. A few days later, the Bishop told the Mayor
of the City:* "Father Janssen, the chaplain of the
Ursuline Sisters, came to me. Imagine, he wants to
build a mission seminary and has nothing
to begin with. He is either a fool or a saint."

De Munt property,
Tegelen,
originally
offered to Arnold
Janssen; today it is the
Nazareth Convent of
the Benedictine Sisters
of Perpetual
Adoration
(Oude Munt)

His Excellency Johann Bernhard Brinkmann, the Bishop of Münster, whom Janssen visited in January 1875, also gave his consent but was shocked when he heard the price of 45,000 Marks. Janssen was depressed. Where would he find the necessary money? The next day on his way to Mass in a Franciscan Monastery, he met a priest from Kaldenkirchen who asked him about his plans. After listening attentively, the priest referred Janssen to the Franciscan Provincial, Father Gregorius Janknecht.

Divine Providence directed me to that priest. When he heard of the Bishop's shock over the 45,000 Marks, he said: "Only 45,000 Marks? That is a mere trifle. It can be raised."

Actually the meeting did not produce any money for Janssen, but it did give him new courage.

He then went to the Archbishop of Cologne, Paul Melchers. The Archbishop was a very serious person who had been imprisoned for more than six months as a result of the cultural revolutionary laws. He pointed out to Janssen: "We live in times when everything is crumbling and threatening to collapse, and here you come and want to set up something new."

Arnold Janssen replied: "Please, pardon me, Your Excellency. True, we are living at a time when much is being destroyed, but that is all the more reason to build something new. When newly ordained priests can no longer work in the home country, it seems to me that they should turn their attention to the foreign missions."

Almost no one had any confidence in the small priest from the Lower Rhine. Father Fugemann, the parish priest at Kempen and the future pastor of Kranenburg, referring to the founding of a misson seminary, told Janssen: "Do it. You have been called because you have: 1, the necessary perseverance; 2, the right kind of piety, and 3, you are sufficiently impractical."

In March 1875, Janssen received his first large donation – 9,000 Marks from the Poor Clare Sisters in Düsseldorf. A second donation of 6,000 Marks was sent by a modest and pious housekeeper. These combined sums were just enough to cover the cost of the first Mission Seminary in Steyl. However before making the purchase, Arnold Janssen set out on an extended trip to visit and obtain the approval and blessing of the German, Austrian, and Dutch Bishops as well as the Bishop of Luxembourg for his new undertaking.

"This is a work of God; you may not give it up, no matter how many difficulties you encounter," *Bishop Konrad Martin of Paderborn told Janssen when he visited him in his confinement in the fortress of Wesel.*

Gradually collaborators began to arrive. The first three were two seminarians in minor orders, Franz X. Reichart and Johann Baptist von Anzer from the dioceses of Brixen and Regensburg, respectively and a parish priest from the diocese of Luxembourg, Father Peter Bill.

Franciscan Monastery,
Münster,
built in 1860/61;
replaced with a new building 1961/62

Arnold Janssen returned to Tegelen and Venlo in Holland. In Steyl, he was offered the old inn of Mister Nikolaus Ronck, which was near the parish church on the Bank of the Meuse.

The property was finally purchased for 10,000 Gulden on 16 June 1875, the same day that the Catholic world celebrated the 200th anniversary of the apparition of the Heart of Jesus to Sister Margaret Mary Alacoque.

Janssen wrote in his magazine:

May the Lord shower upon this new undertaking, which is greatly in need of grace, some of the holy favors granted so abundantly to our poor earth by the Heart of Jesus on that memorable day of 16 June 1675. The mission seminary shall never forget this significant day of its foundation. Its whole purpose is to strive for the fulfillment of the merciful intentions of Jesus' Heart. Through the founding of this seminary we feel all the more exhorted to proclaim ever more explicitly the Heart of Jesus. As evidence of this, we shall adopt the following words as our motto:

Vivat Cor Jesu in cordibus hominum!

May the Heart of Jesus live in the hearts of men!

In a petition to the Archbishop of Cologne, Arnold Janssen clearly outlined the purpose of the new mission seminary:

Therefore, the purpose of the seminary will be to train, equip and send forth missionaries to mission countries, and to act in such a manner that the apostolic spirit and concern for the spread of God's Kingdom on earth may flourish ever more in our homeland. In addition to this principal purpose, there is a secondary objective. All teachers of the seminary shall be given ample opportunity to advance the Christian sciences, and those who are specially qualified be assured sufficient time to pursue such scientific study.

The new and modest mission seminary was dedicated on the feast of the Nativity of Our Lady, 8 September 1875. Arnold Janssen preached the sermon. Among other things, he said:

This is a unique and rare celebration that has solemnly brought together so many of us around the Lord's altar. It marks the beginning of a holy undertaking dedicated to God, which, even if it achieves only half of its objectives, cannot help but be a source of salvation and blessing for thousands of people. . . .

We hope that this seminary will achieve its purpose. The simplicity of this beginning should not discourage us. Even a mighty tree must start as a small seed, and the strongest giant is at first a weak, whimpering child. We know that with our present resources we cannot accomplish our task, but we hope that the dear Lord will provide everything we need. And may He do with us what He will. If the seminary succeeds, we will thank the grace of God. If nothing comes of it, we will humbly strike our breast and confess that we were not worthy of the grace.

Thus was born the Society of the Divine Word.

The Little Messenger of the Sacred Heart
describes the new mission seminary:

Dear friend, do not be shocked if upon arriving here, with who knows what glowing expectations, I show you instead a 46 meter long whitewashed building standing between the parish church of Steyl and the Meuse River. Only 16½ meters of the house has two stories, with eight windows in front. The remaining 29½ meters is a one-storied building with three rather delapidated doors, a few small broken windows, and two large barnlike gates. The longer one-storied section is actually an adjoining building consisting of a stable, a barn and a brewery. Its walls, thin and in urgent need of repair, are about 3½ meters high. They enclose fairly large rooms, but it will require expert skill to make something useful out of them without considerable expense. Far better is the two-storied section; it has ten rooms with two rows of four windows in the front and back. This section will be fully used in the beginning. We hope that eventually we shall be able to restore the adjoining building, because our seminary will require more space as it grows. New buildings are neither immediately ready for use nor habitable.

**First Mission Seminary,
Steyl, 1875**

**Brother Juniperus,
OFM Cap,
Wilhelm Janssen,
co-worker of his brother
Arnold Janssen
in Steyl from 1875 to 1877**

"We live in a debt-free house," *Rector Janssen told his co-workers the day after the dedication.* "But we also begin our life here with nothing." *Even the basic necessities were lacking. In the meantime, the number of residents rose to nine. Brother Juniperus, Arnold Janssen's brother, came to help since the Capuchins had been expelled from Münster. There he had served as a cook. He continued in the same capacity in Steyl and at the same time performed many other duties. It is no exaggeration to say that without the help of this Capuchin Brother during those first years, Steyl would never have become what it actually was later.*

Steyl today

The beginning was not easy. Both internal and external problems threatened the undertaking. Some of the early co-workers left because they did not agree with the secondary objective of the foundation – the cultivation of Christian sciences. Public opinion was really not in favor of Rector Janssen.

Later, Janssen admitted that in those days he prayed as follows:

O Lord, we have now come to that point where once again everything seems to be going wrong. It is up to you now to show your power! I can confidently say: "If this is a mere human endeavor, then its collapse is inevitable. But if it is your work, O Lord, then show your powerful arm!"

He tells of his experience at that time:

I readily noted every place I went that people regarded me with pity as a person deluding himself with extravagant dreams. If anyone is to believe what a man later said about this general attitude, it was one of the mildest judgements passed. Father Bill, after a few months' stay with me in Steyl, told me one day: "I have spoken with many priests in Germany and Holland and I have yet to find a single one who expects any results from this undertaking." I answered: "That is good. If one has great expectations from an enterprise such as this and nothing comes of it, then it is a poor venture; but if one does not expect anything whatsoever from it and yet in the end something comes of it, then one has all the more reason to thank God."

Steyl Mission Seminary 1880; at left, the seminary of 1875 with addition

Steyl today

The parish priest of Steyl had the same negative opinion: "Rector Janssen believes that he will succeed, but no one will ever see anything come out of this whole venture."

And in neighboring Tegelen, they remarked: "This will be a Prussian bankruptcy. They will, no doubt, soon all go back over the mountain. You will see, it will not take six months before hunger will drive them all away."

Despite all these negative comments, the mission seminary grew internally and externally. The enrollment increased; almost every year saw a new addition built. Practically everything that we see in Steyl today was built during the Founder's lifetime. Though money was usually lacking, Janssen had his own philosophy on this point:

55

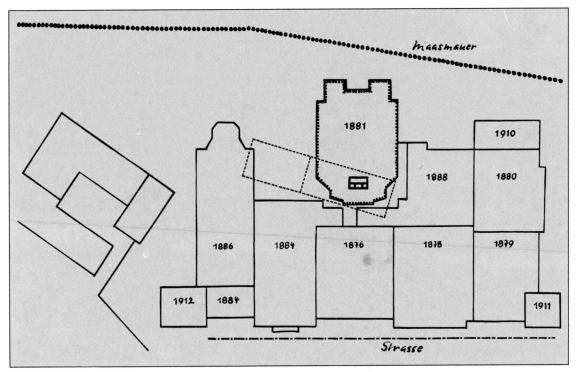

Layout of Steyl complex with construction dates; Scale: 1:1000

Building enterprises for the work of God are a peculiar matter. Those who wait until they have all the cash required before starting a building to be used for the glory of God and the salvation of souls, will only progress slowly and with difficulty. Quite different results will be achieved by those who have courage and confidence. Naturally, everything has its limits. How true the words of that God-trusting Bishop of Münster, Johann Georg Müller. He, who untertook and completed many costly projects, used to say to his parish priests: "Gentlemen, just begin and remember that the money is already there, that is to say, in the pockets of the good people who will give it to you at the proper time."

Trust in God is the virtue from which a missionary has to draw his strength and help. Yes, a missionary must be a true hero of trust in God. Therefore, it is a good thing that right from the beginning and down through the years our mission seminary has been sustained by this virtue. One tends to look for worldly and human support on which to base one's existence, and then all fails. And yet nothing is wanting to him who trusts in God. Has a monastery or a religious house ever been put up for public sale because of a lack of material means? Never! God takes care of those who serve Him. . . .

At the time we first initiated construction, we learned something that has been extremely important in the development of our work. When planning a future building, we never ask ourselves: "Do we have the necessary money?" but rather, "Is this building necessary?" Then, we trustfully and cheerfully go to work, even if only one half, one tenth or one twentieth of the building cost is available. We have always been able to complete and pay for all construction without having to borrow money.

Upper Church, Steyl

One of the main tasks of the mission seminary was to train new missionaries. Hence in 1875, an "Apostolic School," a kind of mission high school, was established at the seminary. Father Hermann Wegener, whose duty it was to supervise the pupils, was its first prefect.

Arnold Janssen justified the need for such a school as follows:

1. a missionary needs more knowledge and skills than an ordinary priest;

2. a missionary needs a more intensive education in the spirit of generosity, devotion and readiness for sacrifice than an ordinary priest in order that he may persevere in his vocation when faced with sacrifice;

3. apostolic schools are institutes where qualified but needy students may be admitted and receive full board and lodging even during the holidays. This is not the case with normal religious educational institutes.

**Father Hermann Wegener,
1850–1920,
first Prefect of
students in Steyl**

5. The Mission Press

Within a year after founding the mission seminary, Arnold Janssen set up his own printing press. On the occasion of accepting delivery of his first press in January 1876 the founder of Steyl wrote in the **Little Messenger of the Sacred Heart:**

Today, the press is a mighty power. An example is the role this magazine has played in paving the way for the foundation of our mission seminary. Without it the seminary might never have come into existence or would not have done so in so short a time.

Indeed, the press can be likened to a sword – a sword used in spiritual battle. A valid cause requires the support of an effective press. An effective press is one wholly owned just as a sword must be owned by its wielder and not just borrowed or rented as each occasion for battle arises. The decision to acquire our own press at this time was a difficult one. But then how many doubts do not foreshadow any new undertaking? Doesn't everyone have an innate fear of taking on new obligations, commitments and responsibilities? But in this case, the very character of our seminary dictated the decision. . . .

The efficacy of a mission press is apparent when one recognizes that every missionary society must provide its members with catechisms, prayerbooks and other printed matter in order to function efficiently in missionary countries. But how can it perform this task if no one in the congregation has a working knowledge of the printing process? The skills necessary to perform effectively in foreign missions must be learned here at home.

This discussion demonstrates the intimate relationship between the establishment of the press and the purpose of our seminary. May the good Lord grant that it may ever add to His glory and be the source of much good. The holy Archangel Michael is the patron of our seminary; we also place our new mission press under his protection. In his honor, we shall call it the "St. Michael Mission Press in Steyl." Through his humility he drove the devil from heaven. He is still the glorious and always humble standard bearer of Christ's Cross. Under his protection and through the humility of the Cross of Christ may this new printing press subdue the pride of Christ's adversaries. May the principles of the saints, who followed Jesus along the way of grace, humility and patience, serve us in battle and become our victory banner.

These principles are certainly not recognized everywhere; their defense will encourage us not only in battle, but ultimately in victory. As surely as the devil will provide the battle, so will St. Michael mercifully guide us to victory.

1909

Steyl Mission Press, Rotogravure Press

The extent of Arnold Janssen's foresight on that occasion is amply evidenced by the subsequent development of the press and its publications. Today, the use of modern communications media remains the special task of Arnold Janssen's sons and daughters. In the same article, he gave the basic reasons for the apostolate of the press:

Referring to the conversion of the world, our Divine Savior called the Apostles' attention to the Word when He said: "Proclaim the Gospel to all creatures!" In His time the printed word was not yet known, but it is known today and the devil uses it for evil ends. Hence the servant of Jesus must also use it to produce good. How mighty is the printed word which the press can multiply a thousand times in an hour! But it is not the quantity of printed matter that is important. What is decisive is that the printed word be read and taken to heart. May God grant that this be so; may the holy protector of our press apostolate and printing office guide us.

Composing room today

1905

63

Erster Jahrgang.
Zu bestellen an der Post, bei uns, den Agenten, oder im Buchhandel.

Steyl, 6. Januar 1878.
Jährlich in 12 Heften, oder 52 Nummern.
Preis vierteljährlich 2 Mark.

Die heilige

Stadt Gottes

ILLUSTRIRTES SONNTAGSBLATT FÜR DAS KATHOLISCHE VOLK.

Nr. 1. Religiös unterhaltende Wochenschrift. Herausgegeben vom Missionshause zum hl. Erzengel Michael zu Steyl. 1878.

The founding of a second magazine, **Stadt Gottes** (City of God), was of great significance. The suggestion for its publication came from a man named Bogaerts, a printer from Hertogenbosch. In 1877 Mister Bogaerts offered the illustrations of his Dutch Catholic magazine to Arnold Janssen for a pictorial family magazine aimed at German speaking readers. Janssen reports:

This offer took us completely by surprise. We were already publishing one magazine which was dedicated exclusively to the missionary cause, and now we were asked to publish another, larger in size and with articles for the most part not related to missionary activity, articles even of purely secular character. At first, this simply did not appeal. Only after long deliberation did we arrive at the following conclusions: We want to arouse and promote interest in the missions. Yet we must realize that those who read the **Little Messenger of the Sacred Heart,** a purely missionary magazine, already have a definite interest in the missions. But by means of a non-mission magazine the seminary and its press could bring the mission idea to circles otherwise not easy to reach. The suggested illustrated magazine would be an excellent vehicle to achieve this.

In addition we were aware that our press was still very modest and limited. We had tried soliciting outside help to produce a matrix (stereotyping).

Although we received help, we were not successful. The advantage for a developing press to be connected with a larger press already operating on a vaster scale was apparent. The profit expected from such an undertaking was also a deciding factor since we were feeling the pinch of being completely dependent on donations. Finally, we decided to submit the entire plan to His Excellency, Bishop Paredis. Should he disapprove of it, we would abandon the idea. But the Bishop did not disapprove; on the contrary, he found the arguments presented so valid that he warmly recommended publication. Thus we finally decided to go ahead in God's name, fully realizing that the publication of this new magazine would be considered by many as unsuitable to our purpose. However, since our Most Reverend Bishop had given his approval, we felt that it was the will of God. Therefore, we started publication, but not entirely without apprehension that in the end it might prove unsuccessful. Also it was a very daring venture as we did not have the necessary editorial staff.

The fact that the undertaking did eventually succeed despite all kinds of abortive performances, and that the **Stadt Gottes** is now the most widely read Catholic illustrated magazine in Germany, demands our gratitude to the Lord and all who cooperated throughout the years.

Steyl Mission Press, Retouching

In the beginning, I had to take over the editing myself. On the front page of the initial issue, we wanted an illustration of the faith in a strikingly large format. I asked several priests to write an appropriate poem to accompany it. The poem chosen was written by my brother, Johannes. When I set out for Rome on an extended trip, Johannes took over the editorship.

Since 1880 the St. Michael Almanac has enjoyed an equally impressive circulation. It was the first Catholic mission almanac in Germany and was published at the suggestion of a convert from Berlin. In 1907 Arnold Janssen took over the publication of the almost extinct **Katholieke Missien** *for Dutch speaking readers.*

6. Mission Brothers and Sisters

The Sisters of Divine Providence took care of the mission seminary's kitchen and laundry from 1876 to 1888. The Sisters had made their new home in St. Joseph Convent, Steyl, after being expelled from Germany during the cultural revolution.

A section of the original text of the first Constitutions of the Society of the Divine Word with the signatures of four members of the first General Chapter, December 1884–May 1886

St. Joseph Convent, Steyl, formerly the Provincialate of the Divine Providence Sisters

In the early years paid lay help was employed in the printing press and workshops of the mission seminary. Arnold Janssen soon realized what a considerable advantage it would be to have workers who would work alongside the priests with the goal of the mission seminary as their motivation rather than financial recompense. This would be true in the home country as well as in the missions. He knew that the established orders had their own Brothers, but at this point he had no intention of founding a religious order of Brothers. Grace and time must decide! In 1878 the first helpers came who would later form the nucleus of the future Brother community. Initially they lived according to the rule of the Third Order of St. Dominic. In 1882 they were given their first distinctive habit. When Arnold Janssen finally decided to found the Divine Word Missionary Brothers, the Brothers requested a position in the Society consistent with their professional obligations – a position entirely different from that of Brothers in the older religious orders.

By 1880 the Brothers, including postulants and novices, numbered 64; by the time the first constitutions were drawn up five years later, there were 185. Their number rose to 297 in 1895 and to 550 in 1900. At this point they outnumbered the priests in the Society. In a report given on the 25th anniversary of the mission seminary in Steyl (1900), it was said of the Brothers: "Without their energetic and self-sacrificing help, the Society could never have accomplished half its tasks."

Arnold Janssen had a special predilection for them.

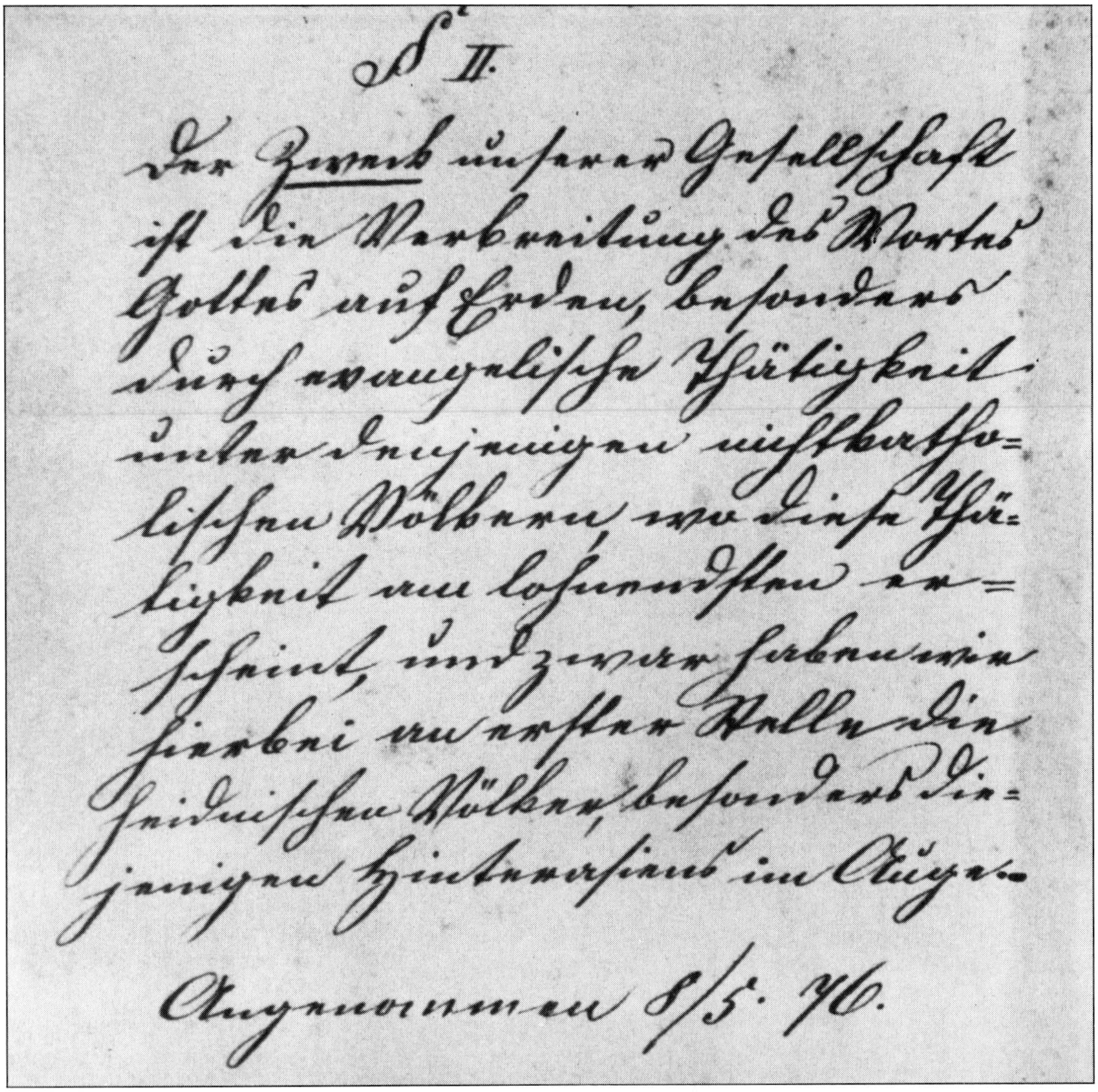

§ II.

Der Zweck unserer Gesellschaft
ist die Verbreitung des Wortes
Gottes auf Erden, besonders
durch evangelische Thätigkeit
unter denjenigen nichtkatho=
lischen Völkern, wo diese Thä=
tigkeit am lohnendsten er=
scheint, und zwar haben wir
hierbei an erster Stelle die
heidnischen Völker, besonders die=
jenigen Hinterasiens im Auge.

Angenommen 8/5. 76.

§ II

"The purpose of our Society is the proclamation of the word of God on earth, through missionary activity among those non-Catholic peoples where this activity appears more successful. Here we have in mind in the first place the non-Christian peoples especially in the Far East."

Approved: 8 May 1876.

A Presentation o the Most Blessec Trinity "Fountain o Grace" from the Main Altar in the Steyl Upper Church It was made accord ing to the concep of Arnold Jansser in 1884

**Sister Maria
(Helene Stollenwerk),
Co-Foundress of the Steyl
Missionary Sisters
of the Holy Spirit,
d. 1900**

When Monsignor Comboni, the Vicar of Central Africa, paid a visit to Steyl in 1877, Arnold Janssen asked him: "Which is preferable – to train our own Sisters for the missions or to get them from elsewhere?" The Bishop recommended that Janssen establish a congregation of his own. He said: "You will then be able to train them for the specific needs of your missions and will not have to negotiate every single detail related to the missions with the Superior General." *Arnold Janssen was inclined to agree but, as was so often the case, he took time to reflect.*

We do not want it if it is not God's will. But if He wants it, He will show us and provide the qualified persons. However, they would first need to be tested thoroughly. For the present we shall calmly await further developments.

In the fall of 1881 Helene Stollenwerk, the daughter of a farmer, applied. She had read the mission magazine of the Society of the Holy Childhood and was an enthusiast of the missions. She asked Arnold Janssen to advise her. In March 1882 she came to Steyl although Janssen had told her:

If you want to come to Steyl, I can accept you only as a domestic and accommodate you in the wing of the house where the Sisters of Divine Providence are living. They take care of our kitchen and you would have to serve them and the seminary. There is another young lady, Theresia Sicke, who has lived here since 1879 and works as a domestic. Speak with her and if the two of you want to live a sort of convent-like life with an appropriate daily schedule of prayer, meditation, reading during meals and working in silence, I shall readily agree to it. Whether it will be possible to found a congregation of mission Sisters later, I can neither promise nor make a commitment. If the congregation should not materialize, I shall be glad to assist you, in as far as I can, to be admitted into another congregation. At the moment I can accept you only as a domestic and therefore fix an annual salary for you.

The two young ladies lived like religious under the guidance of the Sisters of Divine Providence. Later, two other women joined them: Hendrina Stenmanns and Gertrud Hegemann. It took seven long years before a regular congregation of missionary Sisters was established. The founder of Steyl tells us about this long trial period:

Not once did any of them ask me whether she could hope to soon become a Sister. This encouraged me to trust these young ladies, and I began to believe that God, the Holy Spirit, had called them, and through the virtue of silent patience and acceptance produced in them the grace of perseverance. Still I waited until God's will would manifest itself more clearly and until a suitable convent would become available.

The young ladies had living accommodations in a small private house until 8 December 1889 when a more traditional religious ambience was made possible in the former Capuchin monastery about 100 meters south of the seminary.

Sister Josefa (Hendrina Stenmanns), Co-Foundress of the Steyl Missionary Sisters of the Holy Spirit, d. 1903

Within a year the young community again changed its residence to a point between its former home and the seminary. This convent, Notre Dame, was occupied by the Augustinian Sisters who had been expelled from Essen in 1876 due to the cultural revolution. They sold their convent to the seminary in August 1890. Today, it is known as St. Gregory Home with a mission museum annex. On 17 January 1892, Arnold Janssen invested the first sixteen postulants in the blue habit of the Holy Spirit Missionary Sisters. One year later, the Bishop of Roermond approved their rule.

St. Gregory Home, Steyl, third residence of the Steyl Missionary Sisters; Convent in which the Sisters Servants of the Holy Spirit of Perpetual Adoration (Perpetual Adoration Sisters) were founded

It was only in 1896 that the Congregation of the Sisters Servants of the Holy Spirit of Perpetual Adoration was founded. The Sisters wore a rose habit with a white scapular. Arnold Janssen always had in mind to subdivide the Sisters Servants of the Holy Spirit. He had spelt out the mission of the two groups as early as 1890:

The relationship between cloistered and mission Sisters is a parallel one. Both are independent parts of the whole. Mary and Martha were sisters; in the same manner the cloistered and mission Sisters should consider themselves as co-sisters in God, the Holy Spirit. . . . The common and invisible Father is God, the Holy Spirit, the God of Eternal Love, who has called and led them to the religious life. It is by His grace that they have become what they are – children of His infinite love.

Motherhouse of the Sisters Servants of the Holy Spirit of Perpetual Adoration, Steyl, built 1912/14

**Sister Maria Michaele
(Adolfine Tönnies)
Co-Foundress of the
Sisters Servants
of the Holy Spirit
of Perpetual Adoration,
d. 1934**

Arnold Janssen outlined the mission of the Perpetual Adoration Sisters of the Holy Spirit as follows:

What is expected of you is not that you pray for your own little personal concerns. These should be left to God's goodness. Rather, you should pray for the great concerns of the world. St. Theresa was repeatedly asked to pray for insignificant things. But she insistently exhorted her daughters not to lose sight of those important concerns which promote God's glory, the desire for supernatural good and the conversion of the world.

This is what you must pray for. You must be like Moses. When Israel went to war, he would stretch out his arms in prayer. As long as he held them outstretched, Israel won; but as soon as he lowered them, Amalek won. This task of praying is your mission, and some day you will be judged on whether you have faithfully done so.

Johann Baptist
von Anzer,
1851–1903,
dressed as a
Chinese Mandarin

7. Mission Work

Missionary work is the raison d'être of a missionary seminary. Arnold Janssen was well aware of this. That is why in 1879, long before taking over the mission in South Shantung, China in 1881, he decided to send his first two missionaries, the future Bishop Johann Baptist von Anzer and the recently beatified Father Joseph Freinademetz, to Bishop Raimondi in Hong Kong. It was Bishop Raimondi who had urged Janssen to found a mission seminary.

**Father Josef Freinademetz,
1852–1908,
beatified,
19 October 1975**

On 2 March 1879, less than four years after the founding of the mission seminary, the first departure celebration took place. Arnold Janssen preached the sermon for that occasion. With thanks to God, he reflected on the past years:

How many events have taken place between then and now! How many crosses and sufferings! But how many more favors and blessings from the Almighty! How this seminary has grown internally and externally! At that time, it could still be compared to a small, insignificant mustard seed. Year after year it has enlarged its quarters, and the number of its members has grown. If today 89 people – of which 10 are priests and 48 are students – are living within its walls, its success is due to Him from Whom all good things come and in Whom is every blessing and perfection.

Janssen then referred to the China mission:

China with its immense mass of people, equal to one third of the entire world population, is that great land of Jesus' longing. There we find so many immortal souls. . . .

He admonished his first two missionaries of the faith:

You are going to China. You do not know what God has in store for you there. You do not know whether he will make your efforts fruitful. You do not even know whether you will actually reach the land of your dreams. But one thing you do know, that God does not permit good intentions to go unrewarded, and that it is for Him to decide whether He is satisfied with good intentions or whether He also wills their fulfillment. Face the unknown future, then, with confidence. In this dark night you walk hand in hand with a loving God, and our prayers will accompany you.

This first farewell celebration in Steyl was to be followed by many others, either in Steyl or in other places. For 29 years, Arnold Janssen himself witnessed these farewell celebrations as the group of his messengers of the faith increased steadily. In the last year of his life, 80 Priests, Brothers and Sisters departed from the banks of the Meuse for all parts of the world. Like a good father, Arnold Janssen was always vitally concerned about his missionaries and the missions. At the time of the Boxer uprising in China, among other things, he prescribed for the whole Society:

At an appropriate time, in as far as it can be done, a procession of expiation and intercession with the recitation of the sorrowful mysteries of the rosary should take place. The psalms **De Profundis** and **Miserere** should be sung, either at the beginning or at the end of the ceremony. I wish that this procession take place three times in the larger seminaries. . . . I likewise ask especially the priests to fervently remember the distressed mission in their Holy Mass.

Several thousand letters were sent from Steyl to the missionaries during all these years. Arnold Janssen once wrote to Father Freinademetz:

My cordial greetings in the Lord to all confreres. Now that I have a little more leisure, I shall soon write to all to whom I have not written for a long period because of a lack of time. I shall gladly try to console and comfort them within the limits of my poor capabilities. I also have much suffering to bear here, but I try to thank God for it since I fully realize that this is a straight path to paradise and the source of many blessings.

I make it a practice to visit the Blessed Sacrament each evening just before going to rest in order to pray for all our seminaries and missions. You can be assured that China is not relegated to second place. Yesterday, on the anniversary of the mission's founding, I celebrated my Holy Mass for your intentions.

The rapid growth of the Steyl seminary – and on several occasions, the requests of the German government – led Arnold Janssen to consider taking over other mission areas besides China. Under his superiorship, missionaries set out for Togo (1892), Papua New Guinea (1896), the Black Apostolate in the United States (1905) and Japan (1907).

Father Arnold Janssen about 1880

Urgent appeals and requests continued to come from Latin America. When Arnold Janssen heard and read about the sad situation there, he could not resist. There, too, his sons should go and try to save what could still be saved. At the same time, he was convinced that the best way to maintain and renew Catholic life in the homeland was through a true universal missionary spirit. Archbishop Krementz of Cologne encouraged him in taking this step.

Arnold Janssen sent his first missionaries to Argentina in 1889, to Ecuador in 1893, to Brazil in 1895 and to Chile in 1900.

At the time of Arnold Janssen's death in 1909, the number of baptisms by his missionaries had grown in China, from 158 (1882) to 46,151 with 44,564 catechumens; in Togo, from 57 (1892) to 6,163 with 5,052 catechumens; in Papua New Guinea, from 0 (1896) to 1,250 with 220 catechumens. In Japan, his missionaries were in charge of four mission parishes; in Argentina, they did pastoral work in five dioceses, in Brazil, three and Chile, one. The beginnings in Ecuador were a failure and the mission work there had to be abandoned.

**Farewell to missionaries
at the entrance
of the Steyl Mission Seminary**

Steyl Misson, Togo, before 1914

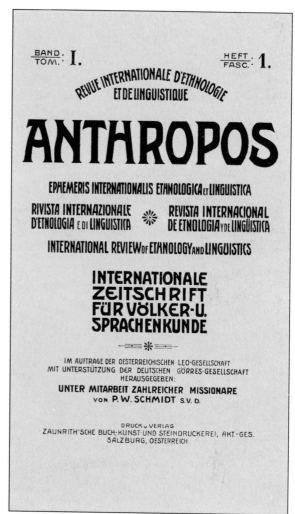

Father Wilhelm Schmidt, 1868–1954, in China

Even during the first months of the mission seminary in Steyl, there were strong disagreements between Arnold Janssen and his co-workers because Arnold Janssen maintained that his missionaries should cultivate and promote the Christian sciences. The future proved him right. The most notable application of this idea is the scientific journal **Anthropos** founded in 1906 by Father Wilhelm Schmidt.

It is an international journal of ethnology and linguistics with articles by missionaries of various congregations and nationalities. Later, this journal gave birth to the Anthropos-Institut whose members are Divine Word Missionaries from all over the world who devote themselves to the study of ethnology and linguistics.

8. Other Foundations

Because of the mission seminary's rapid growth, Arnold Janssen was able to envisage other such foundations. He had built almost the entire present complex in Steyl during the first twelve years of its existence. Although both the high school and theology departments were housed in Steyl, Janssen lacked specialists, especially for the theology faculty. Hence, in 1888 he sent the first two Fathers to Rome for advanced studies. His brother, Johannes, accompanied them as superior. These priests were also to look into the possibility of establishing a house of study in Rome. Such a house of study became a reality; at first it was a rented apartment, dedicated by Arnold Janssen to St. Raphael ". . . so that the Archangel, who restored sight to the blind Tobias, may generously grant the members of the house a clear insight into the Divine Source of all knowledge."

The residence of the student Fathers was changed many times, until in 1928 the Society acquired its own residence in the vicinity of the Ostiense railroad station. Today it is also the headquarters of the General Administration of the Society.

**Father Johannes Janssen,
1853–1898,
first Rector of St. Gabriel
Mission Seminary,
Mödling near Vienna**

**St. Gabriel
Mission Seminary,
Vienna-Mödling**

As early as his second trip to Rome in 1881, Arnold Janssen decided to establish a major seminary in Austria. However, he had first to become an Austrian citizen. After long negotiation, **St. Gabriel Major Seminary** *was finally founded in 1889 in Mödling near Vienna.*

After the blessing of the cornerstone, I took the hammer and struck the three triple blows on the cornerstone, at the same time declaring the seminary's sacred purpose:

"For the greater honor and glory of the Holy Spirit and the God of Eternal Love;

"For the well-being of our Holy Mother, the Catholic Church, that her saving grace and blessing may be brought to the people who do not know Her;

"For the spiritual welfare and benefit of the people of this area and of this Empire;

"Under the patronage of the Holy Archangel Gabriel and all the patrons of the Society of the Divine Word."

I read these words in an emotional but firm voice from a sheet of paper on which I had written them. I thought it most important that on this solemn occasion, I consecrate and sanctify the building by indicating its solemn purpose and dedicating it to the Holy Spirit under the patronage of the Holy Archangel Gabriel. The paper shook in my hands as I spoke the words. The crowd listened in respectful silence, and afterwards one of the priests came and thanked me for the few but moving words.

Thus St. Gabriel with Janssen's brother, Johannes, as its rector became the first mission seminary in Austria. Although beset with much difficulty, Johannes Janssen also built a large church dedicated to the Holy Spirit, to Whom he had a great devotion. He died on 14 April 1898.

Arnold Janssen repeatedly visited the seminary. He personally gave the retreat each year for ordination, at which time he strove to become intimately acquainted with each of the newly ordained priests in order to be better able to appoint them to the most suitable assignments later. He himself tells us:

This is a matter which cannot be decided in haste. One must pray much and be assisted by the prayers of others. After having collected all the necessary data, both oral and written, thorough reflection is required. How much pain I take in order to give my priests the correct assignment. Again and again I consult my notes, study them anew, try to absorb the information. Only then do I make my decision.

When Arnold Janssen died in 1909, the community at St. Gabriel consisted of 30 Priests, 400 clerical novices, philosophers, and theologians and 70 missionary Brothers.

Holy Gross Mission Seminary

Holy Cross Mission Seminary was the first seminary founded by Arnold Janssen on German soil. The seminary is in Neuland near Neisse, Silesia. Its foundation had been suggested to Arnold Janssen by Pope Leo XIII during an audience on 10 December 1885.

The negotiations for the erection of an Apostolic Vicariate in South Shantung had just been concluded. The Holy Father himself had explicitly asked to see the detailed reports of the Propagation of the Faith and our Society. He congratulated me most cordially for the founding of the Society and for performing the tasks entrusted to me by God.

He then asked me whether I would also be prepared to take over a German colonial territory as a mission field. I answered that his wish was my command. He further inquired whether we could consider the founding of a mission seminary in Germany. I replied that the present problem of military service would make such a foundation very difficult. However, the Holy Father thought that the German government might make an exception in this case.

As a matter of fact, the Prussian government even offered the Society of the Divine Word the exclusive right to establish mission seminaries in Prussia and do missionary work in its German colonies. But it was only in 1891, after long negotiation, that the seminary was established as an apostolic school for those boys who intended to later become missionaries. It was a real blessing for the missions. Today, Holy Cross belongs to the Polish Province of the Society.

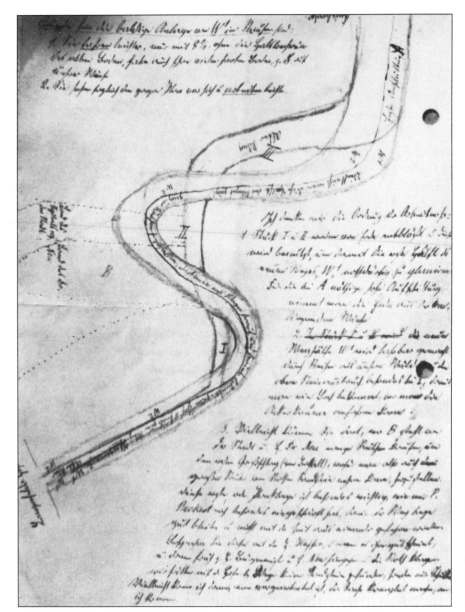

Drawing by Arnold Janssen indicating lay-out for the access road to the newly established mission seminary, St. Wendel, Saar

It was through an advertisement that Arnold Janssen found a suitable piece of land in the Saar valley for a new mission seminary in western Germany – St. Wendel Mission Seminary. The site was a large estate in St. Wendel which the Rhine Province wanted to sell. The first Fathers and Brothers came to St. Wendel in November 1898. The present seminary and large church were built later nearer to the city about a kilometer from the farm. As always Arnold Janssen, like a father, took a personal interest in the new foundation. He even made drawings and drew up plans for the paths in the park.
St. Wendel was a secondary school. At the Founder's death (1909) the seminary had 170 students, 70 Brothers and 22 Priests. Arnold Janssen did not live to see the building completed.

**Entrance
to the former
"Langenfelder Hof,"
St. Wendel, Saar**

Steyl, Kaldenkirchen, 19 November 1898

Dear Father Rector, Brothers Amandus, Crescentianus, Eligius and Fabianus,

As far as I know, this will be the first letter to reach you after your move into the new residence, which the goodness of God has procured for us.

The foundation became definitive on Friday, 11 November 1898, the feast of the saintly Bishop Martinus. On that day I received a letter, dated 8 November 1898, from the Trier Government with the news that both the Ministry of Religious Affairs and the Ministry of Interior had given their approval for our seminary. In addition, the City Council of St. Wendel further guaranteed the foundation by approving an outlay of 4,000 Marks for a new entrance to the property. I immediately sent telegrams to the Most Reverend Bishop in Trier, Steyl, Doctor Kleins in Düsseldorf and to Holy Cross Mission Seminary to announce the good news. On the same day, telegrams were sent from Steyl to the following newspapers: **Germania, Cologne Volkszeitung, Bonn Reichszeitung** and the Salesian **Volkszeitung** in Breslau.

Eight days later on Friday, 18 November, after the departure of the manager, Mister Biermann, you moved into the new residence. May God, the Holy Spirit, the Divine Word and the Love of our Heavenly Father, together with all the angels and saints protect and bless you and give you the strength to lay a good foundation. Externally, you must beautify the farm with its buildings, paths and gardens; internally, which is even more important, you must build a seminary where the fear of God and the true peace in the love of God and neighbor reigns. It should be a place where the spirit of discipline, piety, diligence and patience prevail, where prayer and meditation will be fervently practiced and where silence, obedience and all regulations are faithfully observed. May each one of you support, watch over and protect his fellow-brother and, if necessary, correct him in fraternal charity.

In this spirit, I greet you today for the first time in your new home. I have entrusted you to the care, leadership and obedience of Father Franzen who will be your first superior until an older priest is appointed rector.

**St. Wendel
Mission Seminary,
St. Wendel, Saar**

In venerating the Patrons of our Society, do not forget St. Wendelin, who lived there as a shepherd, and the saintly Bishop Martinus on whose feast day the seminary became a reality.

I hope that Father Blum will be able to come next Thursday, 24 November, and together with Mister Kehl, the district president, settle everything. Should this be possible, I beg you to celebrate the first Holy Mass on Friday, 25 November, the feast day of St. Catherine, and at the same time remember my dearly departed mother Katharina. *(Arnold Janssen's mother died seven years earlier, 1891, in Goch.)*

If this is not possible, then I will personally celebrate the first Holy Mass on the feast of St. Andrew, 30 November, after having dedicated the first residence and chapel.

This might work out very well. If the notorized deed can be signed in Düsseldorf on Monday afternoon, then I will arrive at St. Wendel on Tuesday, 12 December. On Wednesday, we can have the celebration.

Perhaps until then, you will be content with Holy Mass in St. Wendelin's Chapel.

The grace and love of our Heavenly Father, the Divine Word and the Holy Spirit be with you all and strengthen you in the task for which they have brought you together.

Your spiritual Father in the Lord,
Arn. Janssen
Superior General

P.S. Privations, sacrifices and sufferings are intrinsic to each new foundation. Accept them willingly in order that the blessing of God may be showered upon this new undertaking. At the same time, my best wishes to you all whom God has chosen to inaugurate this new beginning.

This letter bears the following personal note of Arnold Janssen:

To be preserved in the archives of St. Wendel as a remembrance of these first days.

**St. Rupert
Mission Seminary**

The last foundation of Arnold Janssen in Europe was in Bischofshofen, Salzburg, Austria. He showed a special predilection and fondness for this seminary and spent ten weeks there during his terminal illness. He personally describes the area as follows:

To the North, soaring high and mighty, are the lofty and jagged Tennen mountains. Made of limestone, they are bare at the top while below spread forests and meadows dotted with human dwellings. To the East, rises a rather steep, well-forested mountain, and beyond that again, one can perceive the distant peak of Mount Hochkönigs towering 2,800 to 2,900 meters above sea level. It is about a five-hour trip from Bischofshofen. The South commands a view of the entire length of the scenic Salzach Valley which is encircled, both right and left, by lofty mountain peaks. Our property is east of the Salzach Valley and slopes gently toward the high mountains.

Though originally planned to house the clerical novitiate as well, it was actually used only for the minor seminary.

St. Mary Mission Seminary

A few weeks before his death, Arnold Janssen approved the construction of the first Divine Word Seminary in the United States: **St. Mary Mission Seminary, Techny, Illinois, near Chicago.**

The Society of the Divine Word had arrived in the United States in 1895 when Brother Wendelin was appointed by the Founder to look into the possibility of selling the Society's publications there. By 1899, a technical school, which was to serve as a basis for the future mission seminary, was opened in Shermerville, later known as Techny.

When the proposal to initiate an apostolate among American Blacks was sent to Arnold Janssen, he was at first unimpressed, but later wrote: "Obviously, a missionary apostolate among the Blacks is a crying need of the Church in America. . . . We are **legitime requisiti** (officially called)."

In 1905 Father Heick travelled from Techny to begin such an apostolate on an experimental level. The Society is still active in the Black Apostolate today.

In 1922, the first seminary in the United States for Black boys interested in the Priesthood and Brotherhood was opened in Bay St. Louis, Mississippi by the Divine Word Missionaries. In 1934 the first 4 Black Priests were ordained. Since then, there have been over 100 ordinations to the priesthood and 107 Brother candidates and novices.

Today, the seminary can count 6 Black Bishops and more than 85 Black Priests and Brothers among its alumni – all Divine Word Missionaries.

95

9. Culmination

Externally, his ambitious goal was accomplished. However, for a person as profound as Arnold Janssen, it was only natural that the internal aspect of this activity would continue to be a matter of concern to him. He spent many hours, even whole nights in fervent prayer. The will of God was always the final factor throughout his life. This conviction is evidenced in a letter he wrote to a mission superior:

Let us firmly believe that the Lord God in His great wisdom and love directs and ordains everything. If we exercise confidence and patience, He will see us through all.

He wrote to another superior:

What you cannot accomplish is not the will of God.

On another occasion, he stated:

It is important that in all things we constantly seek the will of God. This guarantees composure and guards against excessive haste in situations when there exist inherent dangers. One must always remember: If I cannot successfully accomplish something at this time, obviously, it is not the will of God; otherwise He would have provided the necessary means. Patience and confidence in God protect us from excessive zeal and false hopes and prevent us from acting before the opportune time arises.

He was intensely concerned about the spiritual life of the Society. Convinced that only with a true and genuine spirit of sacrifice could the vows of the Society be observed and the inner strength of the Society maintained, he formulated appropriate standards for the admission of candidates. Of the spirit of sacrifice he wrote:

Basic to any spiritual life is the zeal to achieve a true spirit of sacrifice. The Society is blessed when this spirit of sacrifice prevails in our seminaries. In such a seminary the superior's responsibility for guiding his subordinates is simplified. There, when admonitions are necessary, sensibilities are not offended. On the other hand, when people are not trained in the true spirit of sacrifice, there will flourish grudges, slights and the hundreds of thousands of little hurts inherent in human nature which can so quickly spring to the fore when people live in community.

Arnold Janssen always felt himself committed to a God Who was not stingy in His administration:

We serve a great and noble King, Who rewards His faithful servants not just royally and imperially, but divinely. And that is the very reason we should serve Him with a fervor and dedication greater than that achieved by one who toils all day and far into the night in quest of glory and wealth.

Janssen assured that others would not be deprived of the abundance of grace that he had procured for his Society. In principle, all his seminaries were to be available for retreats and days of recollection. During his lifetime alone 5,420 priests and 40,000 lay people (among them 8,000 teachers) made retreats in Steyl.

Arnold Janssen, 1907

**Arnold Janssen
shortly before his death,
St. Gregory Home,
Steyl, 1908**

Arnold Janssen celebrated his seventieth birthday on 5 November 1907 in comparatively vigorous health. However by All Saints Day of the following year, it was evident that death was imminent. He was no longer able to celebrate Holy Mass; his right hand and foot were paralyzed. "The end is slowly approaching," he remarked. " The evening is coming. It is advancing with giant steps. God's will be done!"

As news of his illness spread, letters of sympathy arrived from Bishops and Cardinals. Janssen ordered that letters of gratitude be written thanking his well-wishers. In his letter to the Holy Father and Cardinal Gotti, the Cardinal Prefect of the Propagation of the Faith, he insisted that the sentence be added: "I do not fear death, and I die willingly!"

After a slight improvement, he was able, assisted by one of the priests, to celebrate Mass daily from 18 December 1908 to 4 January 1909. On 9 January his left side also became paralyzed. On 12 January, he received Holy Communion for the last time. His strength ebbed with each day.

An eye witness tells about those last hours:

"The whole of Thursday, 14 January, Father Superior General lay motionless on his bed, his eyes closed. About 8 p.m. the paralysis reached his heart. I began the prayers for the dying. But after about half an hour, it appeared that death would not occur immediately. Half an hour after midnight, his breathing became slow and intermittent; death was near. As we gathered around his bed and prayed, Father Superior General breathed his last and passed peacefully to his eternal reward. It was Friday, 15 January, one o'clock in the morning. We prayed the six Our Fathers in order to gain the scapular indulgence for our beloved deceased. In addition, we recited 50 times the ejaculation "Jesus, Mary, Joseph! My Jesus, Mercy!" followed by the sorrowful mysteries of the rosary. Then, Father Bodems and I went to the chapel to pray the Way of the Cross. In the meantime, the Brothers prepared the body and vested it in priestly vestments. After this, we accompanied the body to the former chapel of the house, where it lay in state until the funeral on Tuesday, 19 January."

Funeral Mass for Arnold Janssen in the Upper Church, Steyl, 19 January 1909

Tomb of Arnold Janssen "Father, Leader, Founder"

The Most Reverend Drehmanns, Bishop of Roermond, celebrated the Solemn Pontifical Requiem Mass which was followed by a procession to the cemetery. The Bishop later described the scene as: "a triumphal procession upon which heaven looked down with complaisance. When we saw the long and almost interminable line of students, Brothers, Priests and mission Sisters, who were accompanying their deceased Founder to his final resting place, the words of Sacred Scripture come to mind: **Opera eorum sequuntur illos** – Their deeds follow them."

His first biographer, Father Fischer wrote:

"This last journey of Father Arnold Janssen through the enlarged Steyl complex was like a triumphal procession. Thirty-three years ago, poor and unknown, he had begun his work here in this out-of-the-way spot. A strong confidence in God was the entire capital that he brought. Yet with prayer, work and many sacrifices he sowed the mustard seed of the Society of the Divine Word, the Sisters Servants of the Holy Spirit and the Sisters Servants of the Holy Spirit of Perpetual Adoration. With tender hands, he cared for and protected that little plant from all storms. God was with him. With His blessing, a work was begun which surpassed even the most daring expectations of the Founder himself. He was priviledged to watch over and rejoice at its glorious development and expansion to all parts of the world. Now he could lay his tired body to rest and go home to his God as a 'good and faithful servant' in the joy of the Lord."

On 10 July 1942, Pope Pius XII signed with his **Placet Eugenio** the decree of the Sacred Congregation of Rites, thus permitting the so-called Apostolic beatification process to begin officially. This decree stated that: "The Servant of God, Pope Pius X, had once called Arnold Janssen a saint. Numerous Cardinals, Bishops, Priests, Brothers, Sisters and faithful concurred in this appraisal. Therefore, the diocesan process was conducted in Roermond during the years 1935–1938. . . ."

On 19 October 1975, World Mission Sunday, Arnold Janssen was beatified together with his first Chinese missionary, Father Joseph Freinademetz. Also beatified on the same day were the Founder of the Society of the Immaculate Heart of Mary, Father Eugen de Mazenod and the Foundress of the Peter Claver Sisters, Mother Maria Theresia Ledóchowska. In his homily during the beatification ceremony, Pope Paul VI said:

"In Arnold Janssen the Church honors an indefatigable apostle of the Good News of Jesus Christ. He was the founder of the Divine Word Missionaries of Steyl, the Holy Spirit Missionary Sisters and the Holy Spirit Sisters of Perpetual Adoration. His life and work, rooted in his profound faith, were devoted especially to the implementation of the missionary mandate of Christ: 'Go out to the whole world; proclaim the Good News to all creation' (Mk 16, 15).

"The great missionary apostolate which Blessed Arnold Janssen created almost totally without material means was the fruit of this personal apostolic commitment and his unshakeable confidence in the Will of God and His Providence. He was a man of incessant prayer, a zealous promotor of the Apostleship of Prayer. In a particular manner he venerated the Most Sacred Heart of Jesus, the Divine Word and the Holy Spirit. He promoted the retreat movement, launched an intensive apostolate of the press and thus made an important contribution to the renewal of religious life in his homeland. The congregations he established broadened the horizon of his fruitful work for souls and transformed it into a worldwide missionary apostolate. . . ."

Final resting place of Arnold Janssen in the Lower Church of the Mission Seminary, Steyl

CHRONOLOGICAL SUMMARY

ARNOLD JANSSEN

1837   *5 November: born in Goch, Lower Rhine*

1847   *Secondary School in Goch*

1848   *Diocesan Augustinian College, Gaesdonck near Goch*

1855   *Matriculation in Philosophy, Münster, Westphalia*

1857   *Natural Science Studies in Bonn*

1859   *Teacher's Certificate; Theological Studies, Münster*

1861   *16 March: Ordained Subdeacon; 25 March, Deacon*

1861   *15 August: Ordained Priest in the Cathedral of Münster; 17 August: First Holy Mass, Überwasser Church, Münster*

1861   *Teacher in Bocholt*

1867   *Director, Apostleship of Prayer, Diocese of Münster*

1873   *Chaplain, Ursuline Sisters, Kempen, Lower Rhine*

1874   *Publication:* **Little Messenger of the Sacred Heart**

1874   *Meeting with Bishop Raimondi, Apostolic Vicar of Hong Kong, at Neuwerk near Mönchengladbach*

1875   *8 September: Founding of St. Michael Mission Seminary, Steyl on the Meuse*

1887   *Private consecration to the Holy Spirit, Lazarists' Church, Vienna*

1889   *8 December: Foundation of the Congregation of the Missionary Sisters Servants of the Holy Spirit (Steyl Missionary Sisters)*

1896   *8 December: Foundation of the Sisters Servants of the Holy Spirit of Perpetual Adoration (Steyl Cloistered Sisters)*

1908   *Beginning of his terminal illness*

1909   *15 January: Death in Steyl*

1933   *Opening of the Informative Process for Beatification*

1943   *Opening of the Apostolic Beatification Process*

1975   *19 October, World Mission Sunday: Beatification in Rome together with that of Father Joseph Freinademetz, one of his first two China missionaries*

THE JANSSEN FAMILY

1801   *27 December: Gerhard Johannes Janssen, Arnold's father, born in Goch*

Arnold Janssen's paternal grandparents: Arnold Janssen (b. 1764, Goch; d. 1839, Goch) Gertrude Janssen (b. 1772, Weeze-Helsum, d. 1828, Goch)

1809   *27 September: Anna Katharina Janssen, nee Wellesen, Arnold's mother, born in Heust near Weeze, Lower Rhine*

Arnold Janssen's maternal grandparents: Gerhard Wellesen (b. 1774, Weeze; d. 1840 Weeze) Anna Margaretha van Eyk (b. 1787, Goch-Lempt; d. 1821, Weeze)

1834   *22 October: Wedding, Gerhard Johannes Janssen and Anna Katharina Wellesen*

1836   *Anna Margareta Janssen (married Lötz), eldest daughter of the Janssen family, born in Goch, d. 1894, Goch.*

1837   *5 November: Arnold, born in Goch*

1839   *Gerhard Janssen, born in Goch, d. 1927, Goch*

1841   *Wilhelm Janssen, born in Goch; 1864 invested as Brother Juniperus in the Capuchin Monastery, Münster, Westphalia, d. 1914, Werne, Westphalia*

1843   *Peter Janssen, born in Goch, d. at the age of 4 months*

1844   *Peter Janssen, born in Goch, d. 1929, Vornick*

1846   *Gertrud Janssen, born in Goch, unmarried, d. 1900, Kempen*

1848   *Elisabeth Janssen, born in Goch, d. 9 days after birth*

1850   *Theodor Janssen, born in Goch, d. 1905, Olfen*

1853   *15 October: Johannes Janssen, born in Goch; 1876 ordained in Steyl and was a co-worker of Arnold Janssen, d. 1898, Steyl*

1870   *21 May: Death of Arnold's father, Gerhard Johannes Janssen*

1891   *10 May: Death of Arnold's mother, Anna Katharina Janssen*